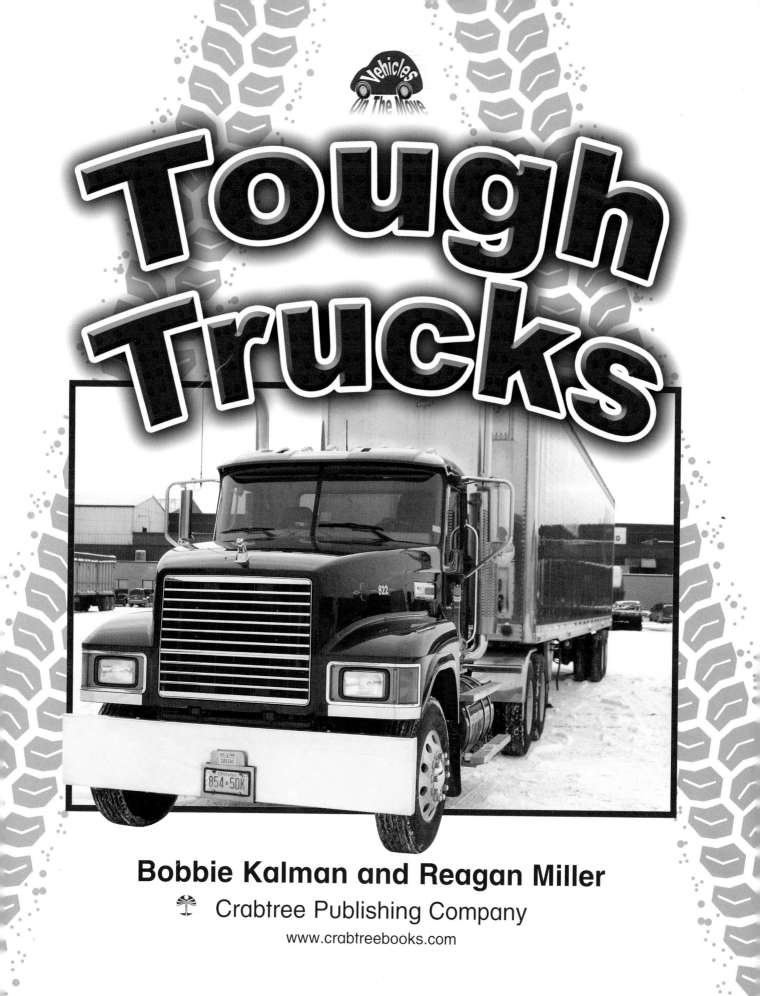

Tough Trucks

Vehicles On The Move

Bobbie Kalman and Reagan Miller

Crabtree Publishing Company

www.crabtreebooks.com

Created by Bobbie Kalman

Dedicated By Reagan Miller
To my brother Matthew and my new sister-in-law Maricel—I wish you both every happiness!

Editor-in-Chief
Bobbie Kalman

Writing team
Reagan Miller
Bobbie Kalman

Substantive editor
Kathryn Smithyman

Project Editor
Mike Hodge

Editors
Molly Aloian
Kelley MacAulay

Photo research
Crystal Foxton

Design
Margaret Amy Reiach

Production coordinator
Heather Fitzpatrick

Prepress technician
Nancy Johnson

Consultant
John MacLeish, Metro Collision

Special thanks to
Bill Baker and Dean Auger of W.A. Baker Trucking

Illustrations
All illustrations by Margaret Amy Salter except the following:
David Carson: pages 26, 27, 32 (dump truck and cement mixer)
Tammy Everts: back cover

Photographs
Matthew Berti: page 29
BigStockPhoto.com: © Robert Pernell: page 11(bottom); © Steve Shoup: page 17
© CAMI: page 30
Dreamstime.com: © John Cloud: page 10; © Chris Hill: page 7;
  © Milan Kopcok: page 27; © Tony Oquias: page 23; © Chris Ryan: pages 4-5;
  © Charles Vazquez: page 3
Fotolia.com: © Robert Pernell: page 20; © Charles Taylor: page 11 (top)
Harvey Schwartz/Index Stock: page 6
iStockphoto.com: page 16, 26
Katherine Kantor: front cover, pages 1, 8, 9, 28,
Shutterstock.com: pages: 12-13, 14, 15, 18, 22, 24-25, 31
SXC.hu/Chris Purcell: page 19
Other images by Photodisc

Library and Archives Canada Cataloguing in Publication

Kalman, Bobbie, 1947-
    Tough trucks / Bobbie Kalman & Reagan Miller.

(Vehicles on the move)
Includes index.
ISBN 978-0-7787-3044-6 (bound)
ISBN 978-0-7787-3058-3 (pbk.)

    1. Trucks--Juvenile literature. I. Miller, Reagan
II. Title. III. Series.

TL230.15.K34 2007   j629.224   C2007-901069-5

Library of Congress Cataloging-in-Publication Data

Kalman, Bobbie.
    Tough trucks / Bobbie Kalman and Reagan Miller.
        p. cm. -- (Vehicles on the move)
    Includes index.
    ISBN-13: 978-0-7787-3044-6 (rlb)
    ISBN-10: 0-7787-3044-1 (rlb)
    ISBN-13: 978-0-7787-3058-3 (pb)
    ISBN-10: 0-7787-3058-1 (pb)
    1. Trucks--Juvenile literature. I. Miller, Reagan. II. Title. III.
Series.
    TL230.15.K35 2007
    629.224--dc22

                                                2007005691

Crabtree Publishing Company

www.crabtreebooks.com   1-800-387-7650
Copyright © **2007 CRABTREE PUBLISHING COMPANY**. All rights reserved. No part of this publication may be reproduced, stored in a retrieval system or be transmitted in any form or by any means, electronic, mechanical, photocopying, recording, or otherwise, without the prior written permission of Crabtree Publishing Company. In Canada: We acknowledge the financial support of the Government of Canada through the Book Publishing Industry Development Program (BPIDP) for our publishing activities.

Published in Canada
Crabtree Publishing
616 Welland Ave.
St. Catharines, ON
L2M 5V6

Published in the United States
Crabtree Publishing
PMB16A
350 Fifth Ave., Suite 3308
New York, NY 10118

Published in the United Kingdom
Crabtree Publishing
White Cross Mills
High Town, Lancaster
LA1 4XS

Published in Australia
Crabtree Publishing
386 Mt. Alexander Rd.
Ascot Vale (Melbourne)
VIC 3032

Contents

Terrific trucks

Trucks are tough **vehicles**. Vehicles are machines that move from place to place. Trucks are tough because they carry loads of things. Trucks carry many kinds of loads. They carry dirt, furniture, food, and mail.

There are seven trucks in this picture.

Heavy duty

Some trucks are about the same size as cars. Other trucks are huge! This picture shows some of the trucks you will see in this book.

Two sections

A truck has a front section. It also has a back section. The **engine** is in the front section. The engine gives the truck **power**. Power makes the truck move. The **cab** is also in the front section. The cab is where the driver of the truck sits.

Carrying loads

The back section of a truck is for carrying loads. The back sections of different trucks have different names. This is a **pickup truck**. The back section of a pickup truck is called a **box**.

box →

Tractor trailers

The front section of a **tractor trailer** is called the **tractor**. The back section is called the **trailer**. The tractor pulls the trailer. Tractors and trailers come apart. They come apart so that a tractor can pull different trailers.

tractor

wheel

Tractors can pull heavy trailers. A tractor has a lot of wheels. Having many wheels helps the tractor pull a heavy trailer.

Sleeper cabs

Sometimes drivers have to travel in their trucks for many days. Their tractors have **sleeper cabs**. A sleeper cab is an area behind the driver's seat that has a bed. The driver sleeps in the bed.

trailer

A trailer can carry a load that weighs 100,000 pounds (45 359 kg)! That weight is the same as the weight of ten elephants!

Trailers carry loads

Different trailers carry different kinds of loads. **Flatbed trailers** carry loads that are long and wide. **Tanker trailers** carry liquids. **Car carriers** carry cars.

flatbed trailer

A flatbed trailer is long and flat. It sometimes carries stacks of wood. This flatbed trailer is carrying a huge load of hay.

tanker trailer

Tanker trailers carry liquids. Some tanker trailers carry **gasoline**. Gasoline is a liquid that vehicle engines use for power. This tanker trailer is carrying gasoline.

car carrier

A car carrier moves new cars from place to place. At car factories, new cars are loaded onto a car carrier. The car carrier takes the new cars to places where people buy cars.

Pickup trucks

Most trucks are **rigid trucks**. The front section and the back section of a rigid truck do not come apart. This pickup truck is a rigid truck.

Popular pickups

Many people drive pickup trucks. The box of a pickup truck holds small loads. The cab of a pickup truck is like the inside of a car. Most pickup trucks do not have back seats like those in cars, but some pickup trucks do have them.

This pickup truck has both front seats and back seats.

Cube trucks

A **cube truck** is a rigid truck. It has a trailer called a box. A cube truck carries many kinds of loads in its box. Some cube trucks carry furniture.

Many people use cube trucks to move furniture from one home to another.

Cool trucks!

Some cube trucks are **reefer trucks**. Reefer trucks have parts that pump cold air into their trailers. Reefer trucks carry loads that must be kept cold. For example, they carry ice cream, meat, and other foods.

Reefer trucks deliver foods to supermarkets and restaurants.

Community cleaners

People use some trucks to clean their **communities**. A community is an area and the people who live in that area. **Garbage trucks** are trucks that collect garbage in communities.

Garbage trucks help keep communities clean. They pick up garbage from homes and businesses.

Keeping roads clean

Street sweepers are other trucks that keep communities clean. They clean roads. There are large **brushes** on the bottom of a street sweeper. The brushes sweep dirt from roads.

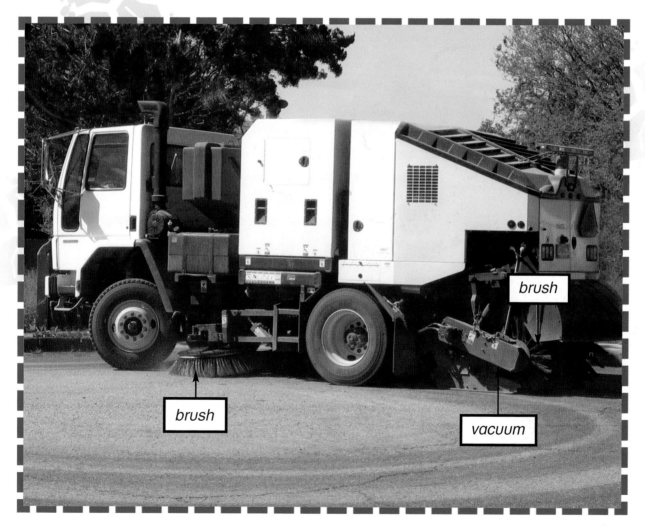

brush

brush

vacuum

*The street sweeper also has a powerful part called a **vacuum**. A vacuum sucks things up. A street sweeper's vacuum sucks up leaves and rocks from roads.*

Mail trucks

A **mail truck** is a vehicle that a **mail carrier** drives. A mail carrier is a person who delivers mail to homes and businesses. The mail carrier delivers letters, magazines, and packages. He or she drives the mail truck from place to place to deliver the mail.

Trucks with treats

An **ice-cream truck** carries ice cream. The back section of the ice-cream truck is an ice-cream store! It has freezers in it that keep the ice cream cold.

In warm weather, the ice-cream truck stops at many places in a community. The driver moves from the cab to the back section to sell the ice cream.

The windows in the side of an ice cream truck open. The driver hands out ice cream through the windows.

Amazing ambulances

Sometimes people get sick or hurt. They need to get to a hospital quickly. **Ambulances** are trucks that take people to hospitals quickly.

*Ambulances have flashing lights and **sirens**. Sirens make loud noises. The lights and sirens tell other drivers to pull over. When the drivers pull over, the ambulance can pass by.*

A hospital on wheels

Paramedics ride in ambulances. A paramedic is a worker who is trained to help hurt or sick people. There are supplies in an ambulance, too. Bandages and medicine are some of the supplies. Paramedics use the supplies to help sick or hurt people in the ambulance.

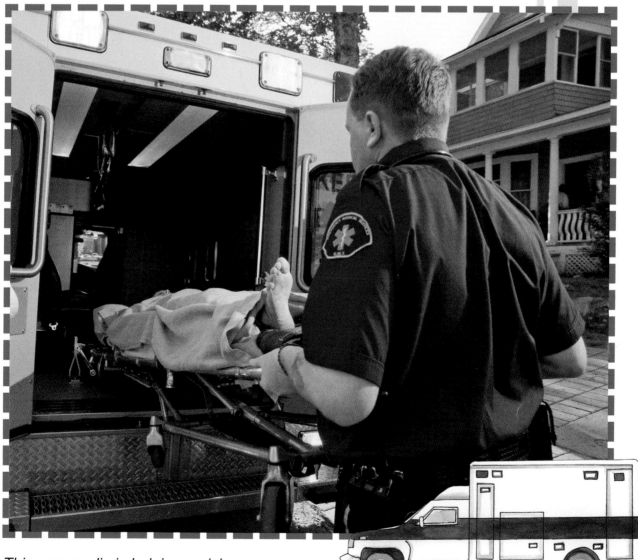

This paramedic is helping a sick person.

Fantastic fire engines

Fire engines are trucks. They help people put out fires. A **pumper truck** is a kind of fire engine. It has hoses. The hoses spray water onto a fire. Water puts the fire out.

hose

Firefighters are people who fight fires. They use hoses to spray water from the pumper truck onto the fire until it is out.

The ladder truck

A **ladder truck** is another kind of fire engine. It is used to fight fires in buildings. A ladder truck has a tall ladder. A firefighter climbs up the ladder to rescue people inside tall buildings.

ladder

These firefighters are rescuing people from a building.

Tow trucks

A **tow truck** is a truck that pulls other vehicles. It pulls vehicles that are not working. It pulls the vehicles off the road. A tow truck takes vehicles to places where they will be fixed.

Parts that pull

A **flatbed tow truck** is a kind of tow truck. It has a large **bed**. The back of the bed can be lowered to the ground. The bed has parts that attach to the broken vehicle. When the bed is lowered, the parts pull the broken vehicle onto the bed.

bed

B-G
Red Oak, Tx

005025469C

Construction trucks

Some trucks work at **construction sites**. A construction site is a place where people make roads or buildings. **Dump trucks** work at construction sites. A dump truck has a bed. The bed of a dump truck holds dirt. The dump truck carries dirt away from a construction site.

The front end of a dump truck's bed can be pushed up. When the bed is up, the dirt slides out of the bed.

Cement mixers

A **cement mixer** is a truck that works at a construction site. A cement mixer has a huge **drum**. The drum turns to mix **cement**. Cement is used to make buildings and sidewalks.

drum

This truck is mixing cement. The cement will be used to make a sidewalk.

Monster trucks

Monster trucks are big pickup trucks. They have large engines. They have huge wheels. Monster trucks do not move loads. People drive monster trucks in races called **monster-truck rallies**.

Monster-truck rallies

Monster-truck rallies are held on wide paths called **tracks**. There are **obstacles** on the tracks. Obstacles are objects over which monster trucks drive during monster-truck rallies.

This monster truck is driving over cars!

Weird trucks

Some trucks are really weird. **Amphibious trucks** can move on land and in water! They have wheels for moving on land. They also have **propellers** for moving in water. A propeller has **blades**. The blades turn to make the vehicle move in water.

propeller

This amphibious truck is driving in water!

Road train

In Australia, some tractor trailers are made up of many trailers. These extra-long tractor trailers are called **road trains**. The land in Australia is mainly flat. Road trains travel on flat roads. They travel between cities that are far apart.

This road train has four trailers.

Words to know and Index

ambulance
page 20-21

amphibious truck
page 30

cement mixer
page 27

cube truck
page 14-15

dump truck
page 26

fire engine
page 22-23

garbage truck
page 16

ice-cream truck
page 19

mail truck
page 18

monster truck
page 28-29

pickup truck
page 7, 12-13, 28

street sweeper
page 17

tow truck
page 24-25

tractor trailer
page 8, 31

Other index words

32

Printed in the U.S.A.